PUPPIES

ELLA EARLE

summersdale

Summersdale Publishers Ltd
46 West Street
Chichester
West Sussex
PO19 1RP
UK

www.summersdale.com

Printed and bound in China

ISBN: 978-1-84953-546-5

Substantial discounts on bulk quantiti
professional associations and other orga
+44 (0) 1243 756902, fax: +44 (0) 1243

To..

From..

Introduction

Every dog owner is familiar with that look. That sweet look which expresses joy, anticipation and a little bit of sadness all at once – never is it more affecting than when it appears on the furry face of a beloved puppy. This book is a celebration of this and the countless other adorable aspects of those little dogs.

Whoever said you can't
buy happiness forgot
little puppies.

Gene Hill

Puppies are constantly
inventing new ways
to be bad.

Julie Klam

A dog is the only thing on earth that loves you more than he loves himself.

Josh Billings

My little dog – a heartbeat at my feet.

Edith Wharton

Every twitch of the
ears is a question
or statement, every
wag of the tail is an
exclamation.

Robert McCammon

Hardly any animal can look as deeply disappointed as a dog to whom one says 'No'.

Jeffrey Moussaieff Masson

The biggest dog has been a pup.

Joaquin Miller

There is no psychiatrist
in the world like a
puppy licking your face.

Bernard Williams

No day is so bad it can't be fixed with a nap.

Carrie Snow

A dog desires affection more than its dinner. Well – almost.

Charlotte Gray

The only creatures that
are evolved enough to
convey pure love are
dogs and infants.

Johnny Depp

Every dog may have his
day, but it's the puppies
that have the weekends.

Anonymous

A dog is the
greatest gift a parent
can give a child.

John Grogan

Dogs are our link to paradise.

Milan Kundera

Dogs have given us their absolute all.

Roger A. Caras

A dog, I will maintain, is a very tolerable judge of beauty.

Francis Thompson

A barking dog is often more useful than a sleeping lion.

Washington Irving

Our perfect companions never have fewer than four feet.

Colette

An animal's eyes have the power to speak a great language.

Martin Buber

No animal I know of can
consistently be more of
a friend and companion
than a dog.

Stanley Leinwoll

Dogs are miracles with paws.

Susan Ariel Rainbow Kennedy

A dog can express more with his tail in minutes than his owner can express with his tongue in hours.

Anonymous

No matter how
little money and how
few possessions you
own, having a dog
makes you rich.

Louis Sabin

Histories are more full of examples of the fidelity of dogs than of friends.

Alexander Pope

Rambunctious, rumbustious, delinquent dogs become angelic when sitting.

Ian Dunbar

The greatest pleasure of a dog is that you may make a fool of yourself with him, and not only will he not scold you, but he will make a fool of himself, too.

Samuel Butler

There are things you get from the silent devoted companionship of a dog that you can get from no other source.

Doris Day

I think dogs are
the most amazing
creatures; they give
unconditional love.

Gilda Radner

The pug is living proof that God has a sense of humour.

Margo Kaufman

A dog is nothing but a furry person.

Anonymous

I myself have known some profoundly thoughtful dogs.

James Thurber

A dog is one of the
remaining reasons why
some people can be
persuaded to go
for a walk.

Orlando A. Battista

I believe in integrity. Dogs have it.

Cesar Millan

The dog was created specially for children. He is the god of frolic.

Henry Ward Beecher

It's hard not to immediately fall in love with a dog who has a good sense of humour.

Kate DiCamillo

In times of joy, all of us
wished we possessed a
tail we could wag.

W. H. Auden

The dog is the most faithful of animals and would be much esteemed were it not so common.

Martin Luther

Dogs are not our whole life, but they make our lives whole.

Roger A. Caras

Every puppy should have a boy.

Erma Bombeck

Dogs are the magicians of the universe.

Clarissa Pinkola Estés

Dogs laugh, but they laugh with their tails.

Max Eastman

To his dog, every man is Napoleon; hence the constant popularity of dogs.

Aldous Huxley

No man can be
condemned for owning
a dog. As long as he has
a dog, he has a friend.

Will Rogers

A dog wags its tail
with its heart.

Martin Buxbaum

Happiness is a warm puppy.

Charles M. Schulz

If you're interested in finding out more about our books,
find us on Facebook at **Summersdale Publishers** and
follow us on Twitter at **@Summersdale**.

www.summersdale.com